Anna Marko

Cambridge English Readers

Level 3

Series editor: Philip Prowse

Tales of the Supernatural

Frank Brennan

CAMBRIDGE
UNIVERSITY PRESS

PUBLISHED BY THE PRESS SYNDICATE OF THE UNIVERSITY OF CAMBRIDGE
The Pitt Building, Trumpington Street, Cambridge, United Kingdom

CAMBRIDGE UNIVERSITY PRESS
The Edinburgh Building, Cambridge CB2 2RU, UK
40 West 20th Street, New York, NY 10011-4211, USA
477 Williamstown Road, Port Melbourne, VIC 3207, Australia
Ruiz de Alarcón 13, 28014 Madrid, Spain
Dock House, The Waterfront, Cape Town 8001, South Africa

http://www.cambridge.org

First published 2004

Printed in the United Kingdom at the University Press, Cambridge

Typeface 12/15pt Adobe Garamond *System* 3B2 [CE]

Illustrations by Frank Brennan
Cover photo by © Getty Images
Cover design by Adventure House, New York

ISBN 0 521 54276 6 paperback

Contents

Irish Rose	4
Haw Par Villa	12
Banshee	21
The Yew Trees	29
Tea	41
A Bed for Ambrose	54
We Will Wait, Too	61

Irish Rose

'You were great, Mary!'

'When is your next film, Miss Flynn?'

'You must be thinking about an Oscar now, Mary!'

The reporters all wanted to speak to her. All the photographers took pictures of her. Her long, black hair and clear skin were every fashion photographer's dream. Mary Flynn, Ireland's most photographed face, was famous and beautiful.

Mary smiled her famous, beautiful smile. She could not ask for a better night. In all her eighteen years she had never known such happiness. First a rich and world-famous fashion model, and now a film star, too. It all seemed so right. It was meant to be like this, she just knew it.

The truth was that Mary Flynn had always wanted to be an actress. She wanted, more than anything else, to show the world that she was not just a beautiful face. She was intelligent too and tonight the world would know it.

It was 31 July 2004 – the first night of the film *Irish Rose* in which she starred with the famous Declan Knight. People were already saying that she was as good, perhaps better, than he was – and he was Ireland's biggest film star. He had been in some big Hollywood films. But it was Mary that the photographers loved. They always did. She could tell. Everybody else in the film was forgotten once she made an appearance. Declan himself knew this. She saw it by the look on his handsome face. 'He's jealous!' she thought as the taxi took them both to the hotel in Dublin for the after-film party. 'He doesn't like the public loving me more than him.'

Soon they were drinking champagne in the hotel. Photographers took yet more pictures for the next day's newspapers. The hotel had many mirrors in it and one was just ahead of Mary as she stood next to Declan. She saw him in the mirror and knew he was the best-looking man in the room, even though he was well over thirty. She also knew that everybody was looking at her – not him. She could see herself in the mirror, her beautiful long hair, her beautiful red dress. Yes, this was her night all right. Hers and nobody else's.

'How about a few words from the new film star, Miss Flynn?' asked a reporter.

Mary smiled. She thanked everybody for their kind words. She thanked the director and the other people who had made the film. She also thanked her manager and her mother. Oh, and Declan, of course. He was good, too. All the things people said about them arguing during the filming weren't true at all. Not really. Declan looked red and went to get more champagne. Silly, jealous man. You'd think he'd know better. Why, he'd even asked her out on a date while filming – at his age! She had refused, of course. Too old.

The director of *Irish Rose*, Chas Gorman, came up to Mary. He had always taken care of her. He whispered in her ear and told her once again she was great – now she could go and enjoy herself and leave the rest to him. Mary knew she was great, though she never got tired of hearing others say so. But now she needed to get away from the reporters and photographers for a while.

As she walked away, she saw a handsome young man with dark red hair across the room. He was looking at her with a smile on his face.

Mary was used to having handsome men around. She expected no less. But this man was different. He had a look in his eyes that seemed to say, 'I know what you want, I know what you need.' His eyes looked deep into her own eyes as though they were hungry for her. His eyes said there was nobody else in the room for him. Only he completely understood her. Only he, said his eyes, wanted the intelligent woman behind the beautiful face in the photographs. His smile was that of a man who wanted her, both body and mind, more than any man she had known.

Mary felt her heart jump wildly. Or was it just the champagne? She felt her face go red. She turned away from the man – who was he to look at her like that? Mary looked again. The man was gone.

The evening continued and it went wonderfully. Mary was busy listening to lots of important people, who all told her how great she was. She smiled and laughed and laughed and smiled, but she ate very little. She did, however, have another glass of champagne.

Mary suddenly decided that she wanted to dance. There was music playing, but it was too quiet; you couldn't dance to it. And there was no dance floor! What kind of party was this? Why was there nowhere to dance? Why was there no real music to dance to? She was the Irish Rose and she needed to dance! The whole world must see the beautiful, intelligent Mary Flynn dance on this, her night of nights!

But there was nowhere. Everybody was talking, drinking and eating, but there was no dancing. It was getting late, too. It was a warm night and she needed some fresh air.

There were some glass doors open at the far end of the dining room and she walked towards them.

'Mary, darling! You look so beautiful!'

It was Celia Jones, a famous English fashion model. Mary knew Celia was jealous of her. 'Ah, well, let her be jealous,' Mary thought. 'She's nearly thirty and will soon be too old to model. She hates me because I'm younger and more beautiful than she is, or ever has been. And I can act, too!'

Celia was holding onto the arm of Declan Knight. She looked pleased with herself. He was smiling like a boy with a new toy to play with.

'You're so lucky to have a great actor like Declan to teach you about film acting, darling!' Celia said while Declan looked down at her with that stupid smile still on his face. 'I expect he's just like a father to you!'

'Thank you, Celia,' Mary answered. 'And you sound just like my mother. But then you are almost the same age, aren't you?'

Celia laughed weakly, then led Declan away towards somebody else. She wasn't pleased.

'That got you, you old cow!' thought Mary, pleased that she had made Celia feel uncomfortable. She turned and walked quickly to the doors.

Mary felt hot. She needed to get outside. In just a moment she was in the garden.

The hotel was beside Phoenix Park, the largest park in Dublin. The hotel garden was right next to it, near a wood.

Mary walked past the people with drinks in their hands, past the smiles and past the tables and chairs. She had never realised the garden was so big. All at once she seemed to be by herself in the garden. But she was not alone – the handsome man with the dark red hair was also there. At the back of the garden there was a gate that led into the wood. As she walked to the gate, she heard music. It was Irish dance music and it was coming from behind the gate. So there was a dance! Why hadn't anybody told her? The handsome young man was close by and she knew he was looking at her. The man opened the gate. Mary knew he wanted her to follow. She did, though she did not close the gate behind her because she had to return to the party soon. But, oh, how she wanted to dance!

Once she was through the gate she saw a light in the middle of the wood. She started walking through the wood towards the light. She saw that there were many dancers there, all dancing to the wild music of violins, drums and guitars. They were laughing loudly as they danced. The women were beautiful, and the men were shouting with happiness as the music played. They weren't students. Maybe they were travelling people who were having their own party. Mary didn't know who they were.

Then the man with the dark red hair came up to her. She asked if she had to pay to join the dance but he just smiled. Oh well, she could always pay later. And he was good-looking, after all. And she just knew he understood exactly how she was feeling. She would dance with him. But just one dance. The man picked up a bowl full of fruit from somewhere and offered it to her. Mary was not sure if she should accept. She remembered how, when she was a child, her mother had always told her not to accept sweets from strangers.

But she was grown up now. And she had never listened to her mother, anyway. She was hungry, for fun as well as food. And the fruit looked so green and red and tasty. She made up her mind and took a piece of fruit, a large round green apple that was heavier than it looked.

When she bit into the apple it tasted sweeter and better than any fruit she had ever had in her life. It was like fruit from the gods. Next to it all the other fruit she had ever eaten was dry and tasteless. She ate it hungrily. When she had finished she found she was no longer hungry or thirsty. All she wanted to do was dance. Just one dance – that was all she wanted – then she would go back to the party at the hotel.

The handsome young man was still next to her. He offered her his hand. She took it.

Oh how they danced! The music filled the air and gave her feet wings. The young man was laughing and dancing as if he did not know how to stop. He said nothing, he never spoke a word. But he picked her up and took her hand and they danced as the wild music played. Mary felt as if her life was meant for dancing, not for the cameras, not for the cinema screen. What a wonderful time she was having! She felt as if she could just go on dancing, dancing, dancing and never stop!

The time! What time was it?

She had not given time a thought. She did not know if she had danced for a few minutes or even half an hour. But she had to return to the party. People would be asking where their beautiful new film star was.

She dropped the man's hand and he seemed to understand. No words were spoken, but he smiled. She smiled back and she left. She could see the gate through the trees. It was still open and she went to it.

She could see the lights of the hotel as she closed the gate. It was strange, but the gate felt heavier than before. And she felt very tired. Well, that wasn't surprising after all that dancing. Even so, she realised she could not straighten her back. Perhaps she had hurt it a little while she was dancing. A hot bath would soon put that right. It was time to go home. She started walking towards the lights.

Her feet felt heavy. Clearly she had completely tired herself out. It had been a long night, even for an eighteen-year-old. People were looking at her as she walked to the doors of the hotel. Ah well – she was famous. She was used to people looking at her. But then she saw that they were new people. They were dressed differently in strange clothes. Perhaps there was something else going on at the hotel. She didn't remember any of the people. Another party, maybe? Nobody had told her about it. Now people were coming towards her. Did she want any help? Could they help her? Mary knew she must look tired, but she could take care of herself and told them so.

Still, she was tired. Very tired. Time to find her director, Chas Gorman, and get him to call for the car.

At last she got to the glass doors. They were open and she went in. What time was it? She had a gold watch on, a Rolex that had cost a lot of money. It was a present from Chas Gorman. She looked at her wrist, but somebody put something like an old stick in front of her eyes. It looked dry, as if it had been out in the sun for a very long time.

But the stick was wearing a Rolex. Her Rolex. She moved her arm and the stick moved. Then she felt sick as she realised what the stick was.

It was her arm.

Mary slowly turned to the mirror on the wall. The face that looked back at her was that of an old woman. The woman's hair was white and her skin was full of the many lines of great age. And she was wearing her red dress. The thin face was looking back at Mary with old eyes that were afraid.

Mary Flynn, the Irish Rose, looked at the date under the hotel clock and cried. But not even crying for a hundred years could change the date that she saw:

31 July 2104.

Haw Par Villa

The small boy could not take his eyes away from the little painted people. In all his five years he had never seen anything so awful, so horrible.

'You see, boy!' his father said. 'That's what happens to you if you steal, don't tell the truth or do other bad things.'

Johnnie Ang and his father were looking at lots of little people made from something that looked like painted plastic. They were all meant to be people whose ghosts had gone to places after their death. Some ghosts were in places of happiness for the good things they had done in their lives. Others, like the man they were looking at, were in places of terrible pain for their crimes. This man was in a lot of pain. He would be in pain for a long, long time until he had the chance to be born again into another body, perhaps that of an animal. 'He was a murderer,' Johnnie's father told him. 'That is what a murderer can expect in the next life.'

The place was Haw Par Villa in Singapore, which is also known as Tiger Balm Gardens. It was built by two Chinese brothers who had grown rich from making Tiger Balm. Tiger Balm was a medicine that people said helped against many illnesses when it was put on the skin. There were lots of colourful ways of inviting people to buy Tiger Balm in Haw Par Villa. It was free to enter the gardens and many people took their children there for a day out. They could enjoy themselves *and* teach the children something as well.

Most of all, these colourful little painted people and animals could be seen all over the gardens. There was a laughing Buddha who smiled at visitors as they came in. There were wild-eyed tigers looking across painted waters at mermaids – women who were half fish and half woman – as well as many other strange people and animals. There were many examples of places around the living world where different people lived. There were also examples of places outside the living world where the dead were said to go. Some of these were very happy places, but others certainly were not.

Some visitors did not like to see the more horrible examples of the next life, but many others did. Some even believed that these little painted people actually held the ghosts of the dead. The visitors usually looked for quite a few minutes at the little painted men and women whose bad lives had brought them to these places of pain. Parents often brought their children there to learn about right and wrong ways of living. Johnnie Ang's father was one of them.

Raymond Ang loved his only son very much, but he didn't like to show it. He only hit his son when he was bad, just as Raymond's own father had hit Raymond when he was a boy. But Raymond also gave Johnnie expensive presents. Johnnie was never sure what was next, his father's hand or his wallet. Today it was the wallet.

'Life is like that, Johnnie,' said Raymond Ang to his son as they looked at the little painted people. 'You only get what you put into it. It all comes back to you in the end.'

Johnnie was not quite sure what his father meant by this but he kept quiet. It was best not to ask. Johnnie continued to look at the little painted people. For them there was nothing but happiness or pain.

The little painted murderer looked back at Johnnie. His eyes were wide open with pain. To Johnnie he seemed quite real. It was horrible. He saw that little painted man again and again in his dreams for many years. He would wake up in the middle of the night afraid, and not able to sleep again.

* * *

Raymond Ang owned several large seafood restaurants in Singapore. He had always worked hard and Johnnie often heard people say what a good businessman his father was. But there was something in the way they spoke about Raymond that showed they were afraid of him. People were always afraid when they saw his father's tattoo.

Johnnie's father had a black tattoo on the skin of his left arm. It was a picture of a snake. He always told Johnnie it was just a stupid thing he had done when he was young. But Johnnie had, even then, heard stories of groups of dangerous men who had tattoos. He didn't want to believe these stories. He knew how afraid some people became when they saw the snake. But he never asked his father about it. Johnnie himself was sometimes afraid of his father too. Raymond was a hard man and everybody knew that. Maybe that was what people meant when they said he was a 'good businessman'.

Nobody said Raymond Ang had ever done anything wrong, of course. People were far too careful for that. No, they just said he was a man who was very good at his business. Raymond himself wanted his only son to own his restaurants one day.

But Johnnie didn't want his father's business. He hated it, even though it made lots of money. As a young boy he had worked in the kitchens. The smell of fish used to stay on his clothes at school. He wanted to study but he had to work in the kitchens to help the family business. It was only after his father made even more money that he could start studying. His father could pay for a good school by the time Johnnie was ten, and he wasn't needed in the kitchens any more. At school Johnnie found his real love – computers. He wanted to get out of Singapore, away from his father and his fish. He wanted to set up his own computer business in Australia.

When he told his father about his plans they had argued a lot.

Johnnie always hated arguing with his father. As Johnnie grew older his father stopped hitting him, but instead of using his hands, he said things that hurt. Most of the time they argued about the business. 'You are my only son,' his father said. 'Yet you do not want to have the family business! Ang restaurants are known all over the city. I made them known. But you . . . you want to play with computers! You want to live far away in a foreign country! Is my life's work not good enough for you, Johnnie? Will my grandchildren live in another country and not ever see their own grandfather?'

* * *

Johnnie Ang grew up and moved to Australia with his new wife Linda. His computer company did well there. Business was good.

His son Wesley was born in Australia. By the time he was four years old Raymond Ang was well known to little Wesley. He saw him many times in family photographs. His grandfather's snake tattoo made Wesley feel very afraid when he first saw it, but the child soon got used to it. His grandmother – dead for years – was there too, in some of the oldest pictures. She always looked tired and weak, like old paper.

Johnnie was thirty years old when he got the news that his father had died.

He was surprised to find how much he felt for his father. He always thought he was too afraid of his father to love him. Yet, now he was dead, Johnnie felt really bad. At the same time he also felt free, perhaps for the first time in his life. Had he loved him after all? He didn't know. He wasn't sure of anything any more.

Now he would have to go back to Singapore to take care of his father's body and organise the funeral. At least they wouldn't argue any more. He might even have a holiday there with his family.

* * *

Johnnie and his family went to Singapore, and Johnnie organised everything for the funeral. It was a big funeral, even for Singapore. Many people came. Johnnie knew most of the people, but there were some he didn't know. One man there also had a black tattoo like a snake on his left arm. Johnnie saw that people didn't speak to that man.

The people who came along brought things to burn on the funeral fire. They brought paper money, paper cars and paper copies of other valuable things. They burned them on a special fire so that the dead man would have the things he wanted in the next world.

There was one old woman there who put nothing on the fire. Her eyes looked as if they were burning as much as the fire. Burning with hate. Johnnie saw her but didn't speak to her. He knew who she was.

Raymond Ang's body was burned soon afterwards. What was left of his body was put in a pot with his name on it and given to Johnnie.

'Who was that awful woman?' asked Linda after the funeral. 'She looked like she hated your father.'

'She does,' Johnnie said quietly. 'She is the mother of a man whose business Father bought very cheaply.'

'Is that a reason to hate him?' asked Linda. She hadn't really liked her father-in-law when he was alive. He had been a difficult man, but he was old and old people can be difficult sometimes.

'I'm afraid she thinks that my father killed her son,' Johnnie explained. 'You see, her son was found shot dead soon after he sold his business. The police said he killed himself. She blames Father.'

'What do you think, Johnnie?'

'I think it all happened a long time ago. My father was a hard man but that's not the same as being a murderer.' Johnnie said no more.

* * *

That night Johnnie's bad dreams came back to him. He saw the little painted man from Haw Par Villa looking at him with his eyes wide open, full of pain. This time the man was real and he was moving and screaming. It was as if he knew Johnnie and Johnnie knew him. Johnnie woke up. He was shaking and could not get back to sleep. He left his wife sleeping and looked at the lights of the city through the window of his bedroom until the morning.

* * *

Johnnie sold his father's business for a lot of money. He knew it was not what his father wanted him to do but he needed the money for his own computer business. His father's friends were surprised. They all expected him to continue the restaurants. However, it was they who were the first to make him offers when he decided to sell the business.

This all took some time, of course, and both he and Linda thought it would be a good chance to show Wesley some places in Singapore. It would be a little holiday.

Over the next few weeks they took Wesley to all of the usual places that tourists visited. He loved them all. He liked the Bird Park in Jurong best. He liked the zoo, too, though not the crocodiles because they looked like dinosaurs.

'There's only Haw Par Villa left to see!' said Linda. 'We haven't taken Wesley there, Johnnie.'

'But it's a horrible place!' Johnnie said, trying not to show how afraid he was. 'My father used to take me there to make me become a good son. I don't want that for Wesley.'

'Look, darling,' said Linda. 'You are *not* your father. And Haw Par Villa is different from when you last saw it all those years ago. It's changed – they spent a lot of money on it a few years back. It's just like any other tourist place now. Wesley will love it, just like he's loved everything else!'

'But those ugly little painted people! I was so afraid of them when I was a boy . . . '

'Your father believed in them, Johnnie,' said Linda. 'You don't. And you'll make sure your son doesn't, either. Don't worry – he'll be fine.'

And so Johnnie Ang and his family went to Haw Par Villa.

*   *   *

Linda was right. It was a fine, sunny day and the place was crowded. The laughing Buddha was there but the place had changed. There were lots of new things to see as well as new places to stop and eat. Wesley enjoyed himself. Even Johnnie enjoyed himself.

'What about the place that you were so afraid of?' asked Linda. 'Do you think it's still there? I think you should see it and put your bad dreams behind you. What do you say?'

Johnnie was, by now, feeling better. Maybe his wife was right. He shouldn't be afraid of a little painted man. He was a grown man, now. He should set a good example to his son.

'OK,' he said, 'let's do it.'

They asked one of the people who worked at the villa if the little painted men were still there.

'Yes they are, though there's more to be afraid of on TV these days,' he replied, and he showed Johnnie where to find them. It was very near. 'See?' said the man. 'That old lady is standing next to them. She's often there with a big smile on her face. It's nothing to be afraid of, you'll see.'

They looked. It was the old lady from the funeral. She saw them, looked at Wesley and then walked away as if she didn't want the child to see her. Johnnie saw her face as she passed. She looked pleased, as if she had finally got something she had waited a long time for.

The little people were still there. They were newly painted but they were the same little people. Where was the little man he had been so afraid of?

'Look at that little man there, Daddy,' said Wesley. 'He's just like grandfather! Look at his arm!'

Wesley showed him the little painted man. It was him, the little man from his dreams. The little murderer. But there was something different about the man this time, even though his eyes were still wide open with pain. The little painted man looked at Johnnie and Johnnie looked at him as if they knew each other. Then Johnnie saw the black area on the man's left arm and he felt afraid.

It was a tattoo that looked like a snake.

Banshee

'It's called *Space Journey* and it's going to be really big!'

Conor Molloy sounded happy as he showed his wife Holly the pictures on his computer screen. Conor worked for a company that made the best computer games in Palo Alto, a city in California. He designed the pictures for these games and Holly was always interested in his work. He had worked on his new game *Space Journey* all evening and she could see, even now, that this was one of his best designs yet.

'We have these five people – see?'

With a click on the mouse, Conor showed Holly five people on the screen: two strong-looking men, a boy, a girl and a beautiful woman. They all looked very real as they moved about on their space ship.

'They're a family who get lost in space and want to go home. Of course, there are all kinds of problems before they can return home safely.'

Holly was smiling. Conor was pleased. He knew that if she thought something was good, it really *was* good.

'Who's the lady with the sad face and the old clothes?' asked Holly. 'I thought you said there were five people, not six?'

'What lady?'

'Look, there in the corner of the screen,' said Holly. 'She looks like she's washing her hands or something.'

Conor looked and there she was, a woman with long

hair and a sad face who looked as if she was washing her hands.

'Well she's not one of *my* designs, that's for sure.' Conor laughed. 'Perhaps someone at the office put her in as a joke. They're always doing mad things like that!'

'Try the sound,' said Holly. Conor usually turned the sound off when he was working on the pictures. 'Maybe they've done something with that, too.'

Conor turned the sound on low, but what came out was something very loud. It was a woman's voice crying out in great sadness, like the scream of someone in pain. It hurt their ears and Conor quickly turned it off.

'What was *that*?' said Conor. 'A joke's a joke but this isn't funny! Just wait till I get to work!'

'Don't worry, honey,' said Holly. 'It was probably a mistake. You know that they're all OK at work. They like you. So do I.'

It was late and time for bed. Holly kissed him. Soon they were in their bedroom and ready to turn off the lights. Their fifth-floor apartment was on the east side of Palo Alto near to where Conor's mother Bridie and his stepfather Bill lived. From their bedroom window, they could see beautiful San Francisco Bay.

'Let's open the curtains so we can look out of the window, honey,' said Holly. 'It's a full moon tonight and you know how I like the moonlight.'

Conor smiled. Holly was like her parents – a real 1960s child. She always made him feel better. Holly was a painter and the place was full of her beautiful paintings and other things she had made.

He turned off the lights and opened the curtains. A

woman's face was pressed against the outside of the window. It was the same woman they had seen on the computer screen. The window was at least fifteen metres above the ground but there she was. Conor could see her green eyes and long red hair. Then the woman opened her mouth and screamed.

It was a terrible sound. Holly screamed too as she saw the woman outside. Conor turned to his wife and held her close. The loud screams stopped. Conor and Holly looked at the window. The woman was gone.

They held each other for a long time, each too afraid to let go, not knowing what it was they had just seen.

The telephone rang by the bedside. Conor picked it up and listened. Holly knew from the look on his face that something was wrong. Conor put the telephone down.

'It's Bill,' he said. 'He's been hit by a car. He's dead.'

* * *

Conor was an only child and had grown up in Cork, Ireland. His father had died when he was ten years old and after that Conor had lived with his mother Bridie. Some time later Bill Henderson, an American college teacher, was on holiday in Cork. He had taken one look at Bridie's red hair and green, smiling eyes and had fallen in love with her. They were married soon after and Bill took Bridie and Conor to his home in Palo Alto, western California. They were happy together and Conor loved Bill as much as his real father.

Bill's death was hard for all of them.

Conor and Holly said nothing to Bridie about the terrible woman they had seen. Bridie had just lost her second husband and they did not want her to feel any worse.

'I will not marry again,' Bridie said in her strong Irish voice. 'I can think of our time together and that is enough for me.'

Conor and Holly knew Bridie did things her own way.

Part of her way was to hold an Irish wake. A wake is a party to remember the life of a loved one who has died. It was, Bridie explained, what they always did in Ireland. She would not change things just because they were in America. A band played Irish music and there was lots of food and drink. Bill was a well-liked man and many people came to the wake. Everybody danced their sadness away – at least for a while.

Conor had lost a second father, too. He wanted to forget his pain for a while. He and Holly danced and danced to make their sadness go away. And, for a while, it did. Even Bridie danced, though most of the time she preferred to watch and remember happy times with Bill.

* * *

It was a month after the wake that Conor and Holly decided to tell Bridie about the strange woman they had seen. It was during supper one evening in late September at Bridie's house. Bridie liked to cook for her family. After the meal everybody had coffee and chocolates. Conor and Holly told her everything and Bridie listened.

'I saw it too, on the same night,' Bridie said. 'I have seen it before. I saw it when your father died in Ireland, Conor. It was the banshee and I hoped never to see it again.'

'The banshee?' said Holly. 'I've heard of it before – my

grandfather was Irish and I heard him use the word sometimes when I was a girl. But what is a banshee?'

'It is a visiting ghost,' said Bridie. 'Someone who has died comes to warn people with Irish blood that a person in their family is going to die. It is said that many years ago, in the old days, people saw the banshee washing its hands in blood before a war.'

'You're not being *serious*, are you?' asked Holly.

But Conor knew his mother. He knew she meant every word.

'You have seen it yourself!' said Bridie. 'It is the ghost of someone in my family from many, many years ago. It was once a fine and handsome woman with a husband who drank too much and hit her. One day she killed him, and then killed herself. A terrible, sad end. Some ghosts become the banshee for their family, just as this woman has become ours.'

'So that's why she looks like you – she was one of your family!' Holly thought to herself; though it was not something she would ever say to Conor.

'I never thought the banshee would follow us to America but it has. I thought I'd never see it again. I'm sorry you had to find out about it this way.' Bridie looked sad as she continued. 'However, the banshee is only a bringer of news, not a bringer of death. And nobody sees the banshee if they're the one who is going to die.'

'So,' said Conor, 'if I actually see a banshee, I'll be OK.'

'That's right, Conor, love.' Bride smiled. 'And you, too, Holly dear: you have Irish blood in you and you're married to one of the family, that's why you saw it, too. But I don't think you should ever let anybody know if you see it again.'

'But why, Bridie?' asked Holly.

'Because, love, nobody wants to know that they are the only ones who *haven't* seen the banshee. It would definitely mean that they were going to die soon. And the banshee only comes when death is close. Yes, I really think it's better not to tell anyone you've seen the banshee. Not even if you're with other people when you see it. Let this be the last time we speak about it. Now, how about some more of those lovely chocolates.'

* * *

No more was said about the things they had seen. Conor and Holly didn't want to think about the banshee any more. Life was good and they wanted to forget about it. Maybe then it would just go away.

Space Journey was one of the best-selling computer games of the year. It made Conor a lot of money, and now he could choose his work. He was soon working on a new Hollywood film. He often worked away from home in Hollywood but he didn't mind. Once he had finished this job he would be quite a rich man. Maybe he would even have enough money to start his own computer design company.

The future looked good.

* * *

Four years had passed since Bill's death. Bridie's eyes were still as green as leaves but there was now some white in the red of her hair. Friends told her she was still a handsome woman and could marry again but Bridie only smiled. She would not marry another. Every day, every moment was important to her. She had lost two wonderful husbands and she still thought about them all the time. But that was the past and the past was never as important as the present to Bridie. Now she wanted to be there for her son and his lovely wife who both meant so much to her. It was her hope that she would be a grandmother one day.

Conor and Holly were still living in the apartment in Palo Alto. They loved their apartment and in the evenings they would look out over San Francisco Bay at the red and gold light of the sun.

Life was best for them all when Conor got some time off and could be at home with Holly and Bridie. They would have friends over or just have a quiet meal together at home. Every new day was wonderful for Bridie, as long as she was with her family.

It was Conor's birthday and Holly cooked some hot Mexican food. Bridie laughed as she tasted it. It was good but it was *hot!* They were all excited about seeing Holly's parents, who were returning from a holiday in Europe the next day.

Conor, Holly and Bridie were all happy and full of good food. Conor and Holly went outside onto the balcony and opened a bottle of wine. Soon Bridie joined her son and his wife to look at the evening sun. This was a favourite time of Bridie's. It was so nice to have a glass of wine and watch the sun go down with the people she loved. It would be even better tomorrow, when everybody would be there. Conor poured her a glass of Californian red wine – her favourite.

'To a happy tomorrow!' said Bridie, her handsome face and red hair lit by the late sun. They all looked out towards the bay.

Then it came in the evening air, just a couple of metres away from the balcony. Its red hair blew wild and its handsome face screamed with pain. It moved its hands as if it were washing them, and then flew away from the light into the darkness of the night.

They all knew that something had happened. Their faces could not hide the way they felt, though they tried. But how many of them had actually seen the banshee? Bridie had told them never to talk about it again. After all, who wants to know they are going to die soon? So, for whom was the banshee crying? Not one of them said anything. Not a word was spoken.

It was understood.

They drank their wine without saying a word and watched as the sun went down into the still, dark waters of San Francisco Bay.

The Yew Trees

'It's got to go,' said Zoe. 'One is fine but two is just too much.'

'I don't know, dear,' said her husband, Rupert Blake, as he looked at the two great yew trees. 'I kind of like them as they are. They look beautiful together, almost like a married couple, don't you think?'

'Oh, come on – be serious, Rupert,' said Zoe rather angrily. 'We're talking about a couple of trees, not people. I only want to cut one down, not both of them. They take away all the sunshine and they block the view from the windows. We can't see anything when we look out.'

She was right, of course. The trees did block the view. They were known to be at least three thousand years old, if not more. But they *did* block the view. Rupert and Zoe Blake had bought the old church on the hill because of the beautiful view of the town, and now they couldn't enjoy it.

No, one of the yew trees had to go.

*   *   *

Rupert and Zoe were well known on British television. They had a programme called *Home Makeover*, which was all about finding old homes and giving them a 'makeover'. That meant they changed everything about the house to make it look different. Old houses were given a new look and new houses were given an old look. It was up to

Rupert and Zoe to decide what the final look of a house was going to be.

That's why the viewers enjoyed the programme. Rupert liked old things, while Zoe liked anything that was new and different and which made people talk. The programme often showed them arguing about what they wanted. Zoe usually got her way.

Zoe was a small woman in her late fifties. She was very pretty, but had a loud voice and she wasn't afraid of telling people what to do. Rupert, who was a little older, was tall and polite. But even he shouted at Zoe sometimes. The viewers loved to see them argue. They made a great team and millions of people watched them every week.

Rupert and Zoe's latest idea was their most interesting yet. They wanted a new home with lots of room. What better than an old church? Rupert liked old places, while Zoe liked the idea of changing the place completely. The television cameras would watch them as they changed the old church into their new home. The viewers would just love it.

Rupert and Zoe had found just what they wanted in Tislington, a small old town just outside Norwich. It was a large disused church called St Stevens, which they had bought at a cheap price. It was over three hundred years old but was built over another church that was much older. Around St Stevens there were lots of very old graves. Some of them belonged to people who had died over a thousand years ago. Right in the middle of the graveyard were two great yew trees – one male, one female – and people had always known them as Adam and Eve.

Rupert liked the two trees, but he knew that Zoe was right about them blocking the sunshine. Even so, the yew trees did look beautiful together. The two of them stood over the graveyard and were higher than the church. The branches of the trees met like the arms of two people over the graves of the long dead. Eve's dark green leaves had round red berries and the two trees moved together softly when the wind blew.

But which tree would go – Adam or Eve?

* * *

'Don't worry, darling,' said Zoe. 'I've got a man coming over this morning to look at those yew trees. He's a gardener from Tislington itself. His name's Mr Ross.'

'Where did you find him?' asked Rupert from behind the newspaper he was reading.

'I didn't. He found me. He just arrived and said he'd heard about what we're doing and wanted to help. It seems that he's been working in the graveyard for years.'

Rupert put his newspaper down. He looked surprised. 'Oh, really? How do you know he's OK? Have you asked anybody about him?'

Zoe looked, just for a moment, as if she couldn't answer. Then she turned to her husband and found her voice again.

'Now don't go worrying about such little things, Rupert Blake. He's only a gardener. All he has to do is chop down a tree. I think you can leave me to organise a little thing like that. Now take a look at these plans for the new kitchen while I make some coffee . . . '

The Blakes were staying in a small house close to the old church. Most of the work was finished by now, except the garden and the kitchen. The house was old but comfortable, with a heavy wooden front door.

Later that morning there were two loud knocks on the door. The knocks were loud enough for the Blakes to hear them from the kitchen where they were drinking their coffee.

'Don't break the door down! I'm coming!' said Rupert as he went to answer the door.

Rupert was tall – nearly two metres. But when he opened the door he saw a man several centimetres taller than him. The man was not young and he had a long brown beard and thick eyebrows. The eyes themselves were a rich brown and there were many lines in the skin around them. The eyes and the face were smiling. He wore a green woollen cap and a brown woollen suit.

Rupert looked surprised and the man laughed a deep laugh.

'People often look surprised when they first see me!' the man said. 'But I can't say I blame them.'

'And you are . . . ?' asked Rupert.

'My name's Adam Ross. I spoke to your wife – about the yew tree.'

'Ah, yes – we're expecting you, Mr Ross. Do come in.'

Rupert, as he always did when meeting people, put out his hand. Ross shook it. Rupert felt how strong Ross's hand was. It was the hand, Rupert thought, of a man used to being outside and working with the earth.

Zoe came into the room. She was happy that Ross had arrived to take care of the problem of the tree.

'I can't tell you how pleased I am to see you, Mr Ross,' she said. 'These yew trees are a real problem. May I offer you some tea or coffee?'

'No, thank you. But a good drink of water will be fine, if you would be so kind.'

'Of course. It is rather hot today,' said Zoe.

Soon they were all sitting around the kitchen table. Ross drank his large glass of water quickly and Zoe had to fill it several times while they spoke. Mr Ross was a thirsty man.

'My wife tells me you have worked in the graveyard for a long time, Mr Ross,' said Rupert.

'For many years,' answered Ross. 'Nobody knows the place better than me. I know every tree, every flower and every grave. Nobody knows them better – except, perhaps, my wife.'

'Your wife is a gardener too, Mr Ross?' asked Zoe.

'We work together when we can,' said Ross.

Zoe looked pleased. She liked to meet other women – she could tell them all about her ideas for changing things. Often she told the women how to change themselves, too. Such fun.

'Will we see Mrs Ross, then?'

'She is resting at the moment. She is very tired. But you might see her – if I need help.'

'Oh,' said Zoe. 'I do hope so. Now about these trees. I think the one on the right, the one they call Eve, should go. That's the one that's blocking the sunshine. We can keep the other one . . . '

'Adam,' said Rupert, helpfully.

'Yes, Adam. Oh, I mean the tree, not *you*, Mr Ross. It's your name, too, isn't it – Adam?'

'I am called Adam sometimes,' said Ross.

Rupert thought that was a strange thing to say. How many names did Ross have?

'But I can help you best,' said Ross, 'by giving you some good advice.'

'Oh, Mr Ross,' Zoe said. 'What might that be?'

'Do *not* cut down that yew tree!' Ross said, loudly. 'Or the other one. Cut off branches, if you must – that will give you enough light. *But do not kill the tree!*'

'Really, Mr Ross,' said Rupert, standing up as he spoke. 'I think that decision is ours to make. I know how much you like the trees – I like them myself – but they belong to us and we can do what we like with them. No one can stop us.'

When Rupert stood up to speak to people it was a way of using his height to get people to agree with him. It usually worked. Not this time. Ross himself stood up and looked down on Rupert's head.

'The yews are older than you know,' Ross said quietly as he looked deep into Rupert's eyes. 'It would be wrong to kill either of them. More than wrong.'

For a moment Rupert and Zoe did not feel safe. They had not expected anybody to feel so strongly about the trees. They certainly did not expect a very large man telling them what to do about the trees in their own home.

Ross sat down again.

'I'm sorry – I'm not used to speaking so much. I really must explain,' he said. 'You see, the trees are really very special.'

'In what way, Mr Ross?' asked Zoe.

Ross's thick hands moved with his voice, as if they were part of the words.

'Yew trees,' he said quietly but seriously, 'live longer than any other tree. Thousands of years, sometimes. And, just like people, there are male and female yews. Yews were special to those people who followed the old ways of believing. Then churches were built over the places where the old ways were followed; this made it easier for people to accept the new ways. But the yews didn't change. They are often found in graveyards – many think they are trees of death. But that isn't the truth: to people like me they are the trees of life itself. Adam and Eve are older than Tislington, older than London. They have grown together, like man and wife, for thousands of years. Cut Eve's branches if you must, but leave her life. Leave Adam with his wife.'

Rupert and Zoe did not look at all comfortable. Before they could say anything, Ross got up.

'I'll go now,' he said quietly. 'I've said what I have to say. I can cut back branches for you, but I won't cut Eve down. If anybody hurts Eve, soon they will hurt themselves. Let her live; take care of her and she will bring you good luck.'

Rupert got up. 'Thank you, Mr Ross, but I think we'd better say goodbye now,' he said. 'We'll do something about the tree ourselves. I'm sure you have lots of other work to do around Tislington, so now you can be on your way.'

But Ross had gone, even as Rupert spoke. They heard the heavy front door shut. The room seemed colder.

'Just who does that man think he is?' said Zoe, trying to hide the fact that she was afraid. 'That sounded like a warning, Rupert. "If anybody hurts Eve, soon they will hurt themselves."

Rupert shook his head. 'He's a little strange, I agree. But I don't think he's dangerous. He's just so used to working with trees that he sees them as people. I really think he sees Eve as a kind of wife. It's sad, not dangerous, dear. Don't worry, you won't see him again. I'll get somebody else to cut down that tree. Somebody normal.'

That night they found it hard to sleep because of the cold. It was October, and although the day had been warm, the night was much colder. Winter seemed to have arrived early. They had to put extra blankets on the bed before they could get warm. The cold wind blew outside their window and sleep came late for them that night.

* * *

The next day they asked a young man to come and cut down the tree. He brought a motor chain saw with him to cut the tree down quickly. But something strange happened. While he was working on the tree, the young man fell over and cut his arm badly. He said he couldn't understand it; he was never careless but he just fell over. He said it was as if someone had pushed him. But that was, of course, impossible – there was no one else around. The young man had to go home.

Rupert rang someone else.

'Don't worry, dear,' Rupert told Zoe. 'Another man is coming to chop the tree down in the morning. I'm sure that will put an end to this stupid problem once and for all.'

'Well, it had better,' said his wife.

* * *

Early the next morning an older man arrived. He had brought a sharp axe to cut down the tree, and looked strong and able. He said that cutting the tree down was an hour's work at least, probably more. So Zoe and Rupert left him to do the job while they went out for a walk.

The Blakes came back two hours later. The man was still there but he had chopped down another tree, not the yew. The Blakes tried not to be angry. The man said he was only doing what they had told him to do. He would not change his story and said he was telling the truth. In the end they paid the man just so he would go.

'What is going on here?' shouted Zoe, more angry than afraid. 'You told him to cut down the yew, didn't you, Rupert?'

'I'm sure I did, darling. But he said I didn't. You know, it's almost as if something *made* him hear something else. He didn't seem the kind of man who would make a mistake like that.'

'Right!' said Zoe. 'I'm going out to buy an axe! I'll cut that tree down myself! You see if I don't.'

Rupert told her not to be stupid. He told her he would ask somebody else to come and do the job. He said he would watch them himself while they cut down the tree.

'You can watch me, then, because I'm going to chop that

tree down.' Zoe had decided. And when she had decided to do something, nobody could stop her. 'If you want to help when I get tired you can, but no tree is going to stop me getting what I want. I don't care how old it is. I don't like it. It's got to go!'

So they went into a shop in Norwich and bought an axe.

When they got back the director of their programme was waiting for them. He needed to talk about some filming ideas for Rupert's new kitchen. By the time he had gone it was early evening.

'Let's get the axe!' Zoe told Rupert. 'Before it gets dark. We can make a start on that yew.'

Rupert did not mind hard work. He often went to the gym and was quite a strong man for his age. He offered to do all the work alone but Zoe refused. She wanted to begin cutting down the tree herself. Either the yew tree went or she did – she had decided.

When they got to the graveyard the sun was already low. The colours of the grass and the trees were strong in the late sunlight. Eve's red berries were like drops of blood on her green leaves.

'Right,' said Zoe as she picked up the sharp new axe. 'Stand back, Rupert; I'm going to chop this tree down if it's the last thing I do!'

Rupert stood back and watched as Zoe made her first cut into the tree. The axe bit into the tree and there was a terrible scream, a woman's scream. Zoe's eyes opened wide as she dropped the axe. She saw a tall woman, with no clothes and skin as green as the yew leaves, step out of the body of the tree towards her. The woman pushed her hand through Zoe's body to her heart. The hand went into Zoe as though it was going through smoke. The hand turned, pulling Zoe towards the centre of the tree as it did so. Now it was Zoe who screamed. Rupert saw the woman and Zoe disappear into the body of the tree.

Then they were gone. They were inside the tree. He was sure of it. His wide-open eyes knew what they had seen. But, when he looked down, he saw Zoe lying on the ground in front of Eve.

Rupert felt somebody near him. He turned and he saw Ross who had skin as green as the yew leaves, and eyes as red as the berries. He looked deep into Rupert's eyes, then stepped back into the body of Adam and was gone.

Rupert heard the wind in the trees. The axe lay on the floor next to his wife's body. A red berry fell onto Zoe's dead mouth.

* * *

The new Blake home was finished. *Home Make*over was shown on TV even after Zoe's sudden death. The viewers loved the programme, though many asked themselves why a woman Zoe's age had tried to cut down such a big tree in the first place.

Rupert lived alone in the church and made no more *Home Makeover* programmes.

The two great yew trees were seen as beautiful things. Viewers and visitors both loved them. They all thought the female tree, which seemed to have grown bigger over the past year, was even more beautiful.

Yes, Adam and Eve were taken care of very well. It was true that they blocked the view of the town but, even so, no chain saw or axe ever touched them.

Rupert Blake made quite sure of that.

Tea

The hot tea was poured with great care into two small fine cups. It was Japanese tea, the colour of gold and lightly flavoured with flowers. Two hands picked the cups up, one a man's hand, the other a woman's. The woman was laughing softly as she spoke.

'Well, Chris,' she said. 'I know you've been here for a month already but let's drink to your new flat. I still don't understand why you're paying so little for the flat when it's in the centre of Paris. But who's worrying?'

Alice DeLancie drank the hot tea all at once, then coughed. It was too hot. Chris laughed.

'You're supposed to drink tea slowly, Alice,' he said, helpfully. 'It's only sake – rice wine – that you drink quickly!'

'Now you tell me, after I've burned my mouth!' Alice took out a small mirror from her handbag. She looked at her tongue. 'Nothing to worry about,' she said to herself. Then she closed her mouth, still looking in the mirror. The face that looked back was friendly with blonde hair and a strong chin. Alice was thirty-eight years old and one of the best writers' agents around. She took care of the business side of things for writers.

Most of the people she worked for were travel writers and among them was Chris Horton. He was only twenty-six, but he had already written two bestsellers about his travels by bicycle in Ireland and Turkey. He had just finished cycling around France for his next book.

So, of course, he wanted to write it in Paris.

'So, how come a coffee lover like you is drinking Chinese tea . . . ?'

'Japanese,' Chris corrected her.

'Sorry,' Alice replied. 'I'll bring my book on life in the East with me next time. But you're writing about France, not Japan. At least, you were when I last spoke to you. I mean, you *are* going to write *Around France on My Bicycle*, right?'

Chris Horton smiled. He was famous for travelling around on his hand-made bicycle and writing about the things that happened to him. His books were funny and described the places very well. Chris was from Yorkshire in England. He liked to look around other countries and compare them to Yorkshire.

Chris was a big man with short brown hair under his well-known flat cap. His face was seen on television travel programmes by millions of people. He was known for the way he spoke and making people laugh. He was the kind of man who liked drinking big glasses of beer and here he was drinking little cups of Japanese tea. Only this wasn't Tokyo; it was Paris! Alice decided it was one of his jokes. Chris liked jokes.

'Don't worry, Alice; you'll see the book soon enough. You know I write quickly. I made lots of notes while I was travelling – all I have to do is put them together. No problem. Have I ever been late finishing a book?'

'No, you haven't. So don't start now!'

Alice knew there was a lot more to writing a travel book

than putting notes together. So did Chris. And Alice knew he knew. Oh, he could make her so cross sometimes.

Alice looked around the flat. It was quite old; the place had been built more than two hundred years before. It was in the centre of Paris, just off the *Boulevard Saint-Michel*, close to the places where painters and writers often met. It seemed a good place to write in. Yet, even though the flat was comfortable enough, Alice didn't like it. She didn't know why. There was just something about it that made her feel uncomfortable. But there was no need to tell Chris that. He would only laugh.

'I'm thinking of travelling around Japan for my next book,' Chris told her as he drank his tea.

'I like the idea,' said Alice. 'But how about writing this book first?'

Chris smiled and picked up the pot.

'More tea . . . ?'

* * *

To: DeLancie@agentsinc.co.uk

From: editor@newbooks.co.uk

Dear Alice

It has been five weeks since you came back from Paris to see Chris Horton. We haven't received a word of *Around France on My Bicycle* yet. We can't get an answer from him. We hope that you, as his agent, might have more luck. Chris, as you know, is usually very quick to complete his work. We've heard he has plans to write a book about Japan. Why hasn't he said anything about this to us? We can't possibly consider another book until he has completed this one.

Please do what you can to get some results – soon! We will pay for you to see Chris in Paris once more if necessary to help him with any problems he may have.

Alice was not used to getting this type of email from publishers about one of her writers. She felt bad even though she knew it wasn't her fault. But they were right; it wasn't like Chris to keep his publishers waiting. Not like him at all. He usually liked to finish one thing before going on to do something else.

Alice decided she would have to talk to Chris again. She wanted to know just why he wasn't working on his book. There must be a reason. It wasn't late, so she decided to ring him. Chris answered almost immediately.

Her conversation with him was over quickly. Chris was very pleased to hear from her and sounded as happy as always. In fact, he wanted her to see his new flat again. 'Just wait,' he had said. 'You won't believe what I've done to the place. It's just great! You'll understand once you're here!'

And that was it. No reasons why he hadn't finished his book. Nothing. Well, if this was one of his jokes she didn't think it was funny! But Alice knew Chris and, he could never keep a secret. No, something was wrong – but what?

Whatever it was had something to do with that new flat of his. She decided it was time for another visit.

* * *

Chris Horton liked doing new things. He spoke several European languages and travelled around Europe as much as he could. He just loved seeing new places and new people. He thought it helped him to enjoy his own Yorkshire even more. 'You always love the place where you were born,' was what he said. 'It's where your heart is.'

But now he thought he was wrong.

Alice was looking into Chris's blue eyes as he poured some more Japanese tea. 'So, you don't think your heart belongs to Yorkshire any more? Is that what's worrying you?'

Chris laughed but he didn't sound happy. 'Oh, I still love my home, if that's what you call the place where you were born, but . . . '

'Yes . . . ?' Alice wanted him to continue.

'But can't your *real* home be somewhere else? Somewhere where you feel your ideas really matter?' Chris looked very serious as he said this.

'Like Japan, for example?' said Alice, looking around Chris's flat.

The flat was now full of beautiful Japanese furniture and paintings. On a wall above the fire were the most important pieces in the room – a samurai sword and knife. They were very old and Alice knew they had cost a lot. Chris had earned a lot of money from his books but he wasn't rich yet. She was sure that he'd spent all the money he had on them.

'They're beautiful, aren't they?' said Chris, smiling again. 'They just feel so *right* here!'

'In Tokyo, yes . . . but *Paris*?' Alice answered, not feeling right here at all. And the place felt so *cold*, though she said nothing. 'What's the matter with you, Chris? These things are beautiful, but you came to Paris to write about France, not Japan! You know France, don't you? It's full of French things. That's why you got this place in Paris – to be near French things so you could write about France, remember?'

Chris laughed angrily. 'I am a writer! Writers look for the truth and to find it they need to be free. Paris is a centre for writers and so is a centre for freedom, where we can say what we want through our work!'

Alice was not hearing the Chris she knew. He hated politics. His books were fun – a good read to take on holiday but nothing more than that. What had happened to him?

'I have discovered,' Chris continued, 'that truly great beauty is easy to understand. Just like this!' And he waved his arm around the room. 'You see?'

'I see.' Alice liked Japanese things but she had never heard Chris talk about Japan in this way before. Not once. 'So, you're Japanese now! A Japanese writer from Yorkshire? Have I missed something here or is this some kind of expensive joke?'

Chris's face went red. He went over and put his hand on the handle of the sword.

'I do *not* joke about my work!' he shouted. For a moment, Alice thought he was going to pick up the sword and use it. She sat back further in her chair, afraid but wanting to know more.

'*Your* work, Chris?' she asked, quietly. 'I thought you bought these things?'

Chris's face looked surprised. He looked at his hand and took it away from the sword, as if he did not know how it had got there. He sat down.

'I'm sorry, Alice. I only meant the work I own, of course. I just like it … I … Don't be afraid. I don't know what happened to me. Er … have some more tea.'

'I'd rather have some writing from you,' Alice said gently. 'Your publishers are still waiting for the new book from their favourite writer.'

'Yes,' Chris answered, his voice more like his own again. 'I'll start today.'

'Promise?'

'Promise!'

And with that, Chris laughed in the way Alice knew and liked.

* * *

To: AliceDeLancie@agentsinc.co.uk

From: editor@newbooks.co.uk

Dear Alice

The first chapter of Chris Horton's book was great but where is the rest? We haven't heard from him for a long while and he doesn't reply to our letters, emails or telephone calls. We must have the book ready very soon so we can get it into the shops before Christmas.

It seems that Chris has developed a great interest in Japanese things. He has even spoken on French television about it. We are worried that his other interests are taking him away from his work. We expect him to finish his work for us as soon as possible.

If this book isn't completed soon, we won't take any more books from him in the future. We hope that you, as his agent, can help.

Alice was angry but couldn't blame the publishers. More than anything she was worried about her favourite writer, Chris. The British public were also starting to ask where the Yorkshireman with the bicycle had gone. It was clear they wanted him back. So did Alice.

What worried Alice most of all was that Chris did not seem to be himself. He had changed after he had moved into that awful flat. Did the flat have anything to do with those changes?

Well, I'm not going to find out here in London, she told herself. The answer is in Paris!

* * *

Alice spoke to Monsieur Dupont, who owned Chris's flat. She found him very helpful. He said the flat was cheap because nobody ever stayed in it very long and any money from the flat was better than none.

'What's wrong with the place?' she asked.

'Nothing,' said Dupont. 'It's just that people don't like to stay in a place where a man has killed himself.'

'Killed himself . . . ?'

'Yes, it was quite a few years ago, in the 1960s,' Dupont told her. 'A young Japanese painter wanted people in Europe to take his work seriously. He was fed up with people seeing him as Japanese first and a painter second. He had a strange way of showing it. He invited a lot of important people to the flat for a cup of tea and to see his work. Then he cut his stomach open with a knife. It's an old Japanese way of saying you really don't like how things are going – I think they call it *seppuku*. Most unfortunate.'

'Did people talk about what he did?'

'No, not really. A few words in the newspaper, that's all.' Monsieur Dupont looked sad. 'He was just seen as a mad young man who was best forgotten. There were plenty of mad people around then. As now. Things never change!'

'So you think he was mad?'

'Who knows? I can understand what he meant,' said Dupont. 'After all, he may have used old ways of working, but he *did* have new things to say. But it was Paris in the sixties. People didn't want old ways of doing things – they wanted change. Can we have old ways *and* change? He thought so.'

'And so he used traditional *seppuku* to bring change,' Alice added. 'Only it didn't – it just brought his own death. So where is his work now?'

'The young man owed me money. So I took his work after his death. I own most of it now,' said Dupont, 'except for the ones your writer friend bought. He chose the best pieces, too.'

'Chris Horton bought them from *you*?'

'Didn't you know? I showed him some pieces shortly after he moved in. I didn't tell him about the young man killing himself, though. No need for that. Oh yes, it wasn't long before he wanted to buy them. He loved all the pieces, but you could see he thought there was something special about the sword.'

'The sword?'

'Yes, and a large knife. They were very old. Probably been in the artist's family for many years. They're still very sharp too. Our young painter used the same knife to kill himself, but I didn't say that, of course. Your Monsieur

Horton paid a lot of money for them, though they were worth every euro, of course.'

'Of course,' said Alice. 'And you have the rest of this artist's work. What did you say his name was?'

'Didn't I tell you his name?' Dupont asked. 'Yes, I have about twenty pieces of work left. He just called himself Zen. Not his real name but that's all he would answer to. No family either – all died in the war. Just him left. Now he's gone, too.'

Alice hoped that was true but didn't say so. 'Tell me, monsieur, when did Zen kill himself?'

'On 7 October 1966. He was only twenty-six when he died. I still think of him on that day every year. In fact, that's only two weeks from now. Ha! How time flies!'

* * *

Alice returned home the next day. Her other writers kept her busy and pushed her worries about Chris to the back of her mind.

A week passed and she received an invitation from Chris. It was printed on a card with a Japanese picture on it. The invitation was *not* because he had completed his book as she had hoped. It was for a cup of tea and a look at his Japanese paintings. It was going to be on 7 October at his flat.

The invitation ended: 'Chris '*Zen'* Horton'.

* * *

Alice soon found out that many television and newspaper reporters had been invited, too. Quite a crowd. People were interested in this English writer who seemed to have suddenly fallen in love with all things Japanese. It was a good story – newspapers loved this kind of thing. Alice was sure they would be just like the crowd who had seen Zen at his tea party all those years ago.

That was what worried Alice. She remembered how strange Chris had been when she last saw him. It wasn't like him but it *was* like the angry young man who called himself Zen. It was almost as if Zen was making his anger known again through Chris. Had Zen got into Chris's head? Could such things really happen?

Alice was not the kind of woman to believe in ghosts. However, she did believe it was better to be safe than sorry. She thought about Zen and the reasons for his *seppuku*. Knowing why he had killed himself could help explain the strange way Chris was acting. Chris, though he would never say so, had always had a soft centre – perhaps soft enough for an angry ghost to get inside.

But was there anything she could do about it? Maybe there was.

The next few days were full of telephone calls, emails and meetings. Alice had never been so busy before in her life. She did everything she could to get some other important people to come to Chris's Japanese tea party – people who knew a lot more about painting than newspaper reporters. It was very tiring but at last everything was ready – she hoped.

* * *

Chris's flat was not large but it did have one big room. All of Chris's Japanese things were there and the room was full of people. Monsieur Dupont and Alice were talking together. Everybody was drinking Japanese tea. The sound of a small bell filled the room. Chris was going to speak and stood at the head of the room by a table where his samurai sword and knife rested.

'Ladies and gentlemen,' he began, and his voice seemed to have changed from its normal Yorkshire accent to something else that was hard and angry. 'I have asked you all here to see the beauty of traditional Japanese painting. This art still has much to say about freedom and change, though I know you think differently. Well, I am going to show you in a traditional Japanese way just how strongly I disagree!' Chris reached for the large knife. He held it with both hands close to his stomach. The room went cold.

Alice was terribly afraid. It was the knife! It was the same knife that Zen had used to kill himself all those years ago. Was the ghost of Zen going to make Chris do *seppuku*?

'One moment, Monsieur Horton!' A well-dressed man with very short hair and a long moustache stepped in front of Chris. Everybody knew the speaker: it was Rousseau, the famous Parisian writer. Chris still had the knife in his hand, but he stopped and listened.

'I am not here to disagree with you! This work may be traditional,' said Rousseau, 'but it is more exciting and says more than anything else I have seen for years! Monsieur Zen uses tradition to free his painting from the mistakes of the past and shows us the future! This new work we see here today shows us the truth about Monsieur Zen. He was a great man and I think we should show his work here in Paris!'

Chris '*Zen'* Horton at first looked lost, then gave a wide

smile. The knife dropped from his hands onto the floor. Everybody in the room smiled.

* * *

'I don't know what happened to me!'

Chris was sitting next to Alice drinking hot black coffee.

'I couldn't help it – one minute I was so angry I wanted to kill myself, then that Rousseau man said how much he loved Zen's work. All at once I felt happy and just wanted to sleep. It was as if a great weight had fallen from me. I don't know if this *Zen* person had anything to do with it.'

'Maybe,' said Alice. 'I thought you – or rather, *Zen* – might try something stupid with that knife. *Zen* was so angry that his work was not understood. I asked Rousseau to come and made sure he saw some of Zen's work earlier on, thanks to your Monsieur Dupont. Rousseau loved it. It seemed to me that once people saw Zen as a great painter he would have no reason to be angry any more. He wouldn't need to show it through you. Anyway, you seem OK now, thank goodness. The TV people loved it all, of course! Do you still want to talk to them about Japanese art, Mr Chris '*Zen*' Horton?'

'No,' Chris said with feeling. 'Tell them to go away – I just want to finish my book! And don't call me Zen!'

Alice smiled. The room, she felt, was warmer already.

A Bed for Ambrose

When Ambrose looked down from above the table he saw his own body lying below him.

It was a young body, only twenty-five years of age. Dark hair could still be seen under the plastic on its head. The face was handsome. There it was, lying on an operating table in a hospital in Perth, Western Australia.

The surgeon was busy. Nurses held things for her. One nurse looked like he was about to fall asleep. Then there was a long, high sound from a machine.

'He's dying!' said the surgeon. 'Give him more drugs, quick!'

The nurse suddenly sat up. More drugs were given to the body.

Nothing happened. The long, high sound continued.

Ambrose looked down, not able to believe what he was seeing. People were running around his body. They were trying to stop him dying. Yet here he was, looking down at them from above the operating table. Was this what it was like to be dead? He didn't feel afraid. All the same, it wasn't what he expected. He had always thought death was the end of everything. Like falling asleep and having no dreams, just blackness.

'It's no good,' said the surgeon. 'We'll have to start his heart again. Get the machine.'

Ambrose, from his place above the table, saw nurses running towards a smaller table by the wall. A male nurse dropped something; it was a gold watch which had fallen from his wrist. The nurse didn't see it fall to the floor. But Ambrose did. A foot kicked the watch under a cupboard while they were hurrying about.

Ambrose saw it. He heard them talking, too.

'He's not going to live, Jack,' said one nurse.

'Don't say that, Harry,' said the nurse called Jack. 'Just hurry up and get this machine started!'

The surgeon put two parts of the machine on either side of Ambrose's chest.

Ambrose felt happy. He looked up, away from his body. There was a light somewhere. It was coming towards him. He thought he saw his mother looking at him from the light. She had the sad look on her face he had seen so many times before. But his mother was dead. Ambrose didn't care. Everything was fine. He looked back towards the room. He saw that the surgeon had a small dark area like a little star on the back of her neck. He saw it all so clearly. He wasn't afraid at all. He turned to the light again and to his mother, whose eyes were now wet with tears. It all felt so right.

'Right – NOW!'

As soon as the surgeon said this Ambrose felt himself falling down very quickly. There was something that felt like fire in his chest. It wasn't a nice feeling. The nice light was gone. His mother was gone. Nothingness.

* * *

Ambrose opened his eyes. He was in a hospital bed. It was hot. Perth, Australia is a hot place in summer, but it was hotter than usual. He opened his eyes. The first thing he saw was a woman smiling and standing next to his bed. She was a nurse and she looked rather like his mother. It wasn't his mother, of course. The nurse didn't have his mother's usual sad look on her face. She looked hungry, like she was impatient to begin a tasty meal. He didn't like it.

'Hi, stranger!' said the nurse. 'How are you feeling?'

Ambrose felt sick. He also felt a terrible pain in his side. Were they giving him something for it? It felt like the pain could be a lot worse.

'I'm feeling … awful,' said Ambrose. 'My chest hurts; I've got a bad headache and I feel sick. Can't you do something about it?'

'There's no escaping the pain,' said the nurse. 'But we're taking care of you, I promise. The surgeon said your operation, went very well and … '

'Now wait a minute!' Ambrose told the nurse. 'I nearly died on that operating table! The surgeon saved me because she used that machine. In fact, I think I did die for a while. I'm sure of it – oh!'

Ambrose had to stop talking then; his chest hurt too much. But the nurse was patient and stood next to him while the worst of the pain passed.

Ambrose didn't like the nurse. She was still smiling. 'Smiling too much,' Ambrose thought. It made him feel uncomfortable.

'So, what happened?' Ambrose asked. He didn't know how he had got into hospital. He couldn't remember. 'How did I get here?'

The nurse smiled even more widely. 'You were shot. Don't you remember?'

Then Ambrose remembered the gun. Yes, he *had* a gun. Yes, now he remembered: the gun was part of his job. He needed it. He was used to guns.

'But we'll take care of you,' said the nurse. 'Don't you worry about anything.'

The nurse's words didn't make Ambrose feel any better. There was something about the nurse he didn't like. It was partly because the nurse looked like his mother. Ambrose didn't like to think about his mother. He was starting to remember things. His mother had begun to ask questions about his job. He had never told her about what he did. Why should he? It was, after all, his choice. It was a job he was good at and it paid a lot of money.

Ambrose shot people for money and he was never short of work. Anyway, he enjoyed killing people and he was one of the best.

Only this time somebody shot back.

Usually, people didn't even know Ambrose was there when his bullet hit them. Ambrose's mother, for example, had found his gun the other day. She might have told someone, so she had to go. He shot her once while she was asleep. She never knew anything about it.

But *this* person shot back. Yes, he remembered the man turning around when his own gun didn't work. Ambrose was looking at it when the man shot him. He remembered the smoke from the man's gun and the blood and the pain in his chest. Then, the next thing he knew, there he was in hospital looking down from above the operating table.

Oh well, he was OK now. It looked like he was in a good hospital, too. Somebody was helping him, that was for sure. Well, he was one of the best killers around – far too good to lose. Maybe somebody else had killed the man. He didn't know. He couldn't remember.

But he hadn't forgotten the feeling that he was out of his body. He was sure that he had died, if only for a short while. He was pleased to be alive now and back in his body but he needed to talk about what had happened on the operating table. He remembered reading about such things in a magazine once. People came out of their bodies during a hospital operation and looked down at themselves. They said they saw everything around them while they were having the operation. They said they remembered everything they saw. Just like he had. Only they said it changed their lives and made them better people.

So what about the things he had seen? Had he really seen the nurse drop that watch? And what about the star on the back of the surgeon's neck? It was all too real to be a dream.

Then Ambrose had a thought. Maybe it could change his life, too. Perhaps it was time to change his ways. He wasn't such a bad person. There was time. He was young. Maybe there was more to life than he thought. He just had to find out.

However, what he wanted now more than anything else was to tell somebody about what had happened – but who?

The smiling nurse was still there. Oh, well – she was better than nobody.

He told her about being out of his body, about the nurses and the surgeon.

'Oh, yes,' said the nurse. 'It's not unusual for people to

feel this kind of thing during an operation. You're not the first, you know.'

Ambrose asked if he could see the nurses and the surgeon. He wanted to see if he really had seen the male nurse's watch drop to the floor and if the surgeon really had a star on the back of her neck.

'That's not possible,' the nurse told him.

'But they were there!' said Ambrose. 'I *know* they were! They must be around here somewhere. You have to find them for me, can't you see? You have to!'

'Now don't get angry, dear,' said the nurse, still smiling. 'You can't see them. You won't see them here. They don't belong here.'

'But I saw them!' Ambrose cried. 'Didn't I . . . ?'

'Yes, you did,' the nurse answered. 'You saw them trying to stop you dying. Everything you saw was real. Your mother was real. *This* is real. That's how we like it. We want you to feel everything. You'll get better very quickly, you'll see.'

'Real? Of course this was all real,' thought Ambrose. 'What was this woman talking about?'

'You'll soon find out,' said the nurse, as if hearing Ambrose's thoughts. 'You'll get better and we'll let you go outside. Then you'll feel more bullets. Oh, you'll feel lots of those. And you'll never know where they come from. Or when. Oh, yes. It's only fair, isn't it?'

'Get me out of here!' shouted Ambrose. 'Somebody help! This woman's trying to kill me!'

The nurse carried on smiling. 'Nobody's trying to kill you, Ambrose.'

'No . . . ?'

'No,' said the nurse. 'The machine didn't work. We can't kill you, you see. Not now. Oh, no.'

And the nurse that looked like his mother smiled widely and slowly licked her lips with her long, green tongue.

We Will Wait, Too

When writers write, what happens?

We happen.

And who are we? We are the characters you read about in stories. Writers make us. We are born in the minds of writers. Writers may take a long time to decide what kind of characters we will be. We may be young or old, good or bad, clever or stupid, men or women. But once we are on the page we belong to everybody. Every reader sees us in his or her own way. We do not only belong to the writer. We have a new life of our own.

We are free.

But what happens when writers think up characters but don't use them in their stories? What happens when writers decide to cut characters out of a story? Where do we go? Once we are born in the head of a writer, we cannot be unborn, just as a thought cannot be unthought. We want to be free. We want writers to give us life.

So where do we go?

We all wait for someone to put us in a story. But where? We wait near writers when they write. We crowd around them, shouting in their ears that we want them to give us life on the page.

When writers think they have a new idea they call it inspiration. If they only knew their new ideas are often us, the ghosts of unborn characters, who have walked into their thoughts. We are ghosts who want to live through their stories.

So, writers, let us live! Go on writing. Your readers are waiting.

We will wait, too.

Cambridge English Readers

Look out for other titles in the series:

Level 3

The Lahti File
by Richard MacAndrew

Hundreds of dead fish. Some unexplained deaths. A birdless town. 'Foreign Executive' Ian Munro is sent to the town of Lahti in Finland to look for answers and discovers a poisonous secret.

How I Met Myself
by David A. Hill

In a dark street in Budapest, John Taylor meets someone who changes his life. But who is this man? And what is he trying to tell John?

Eye of the Storm
by Mandy Loader

In Florida, a man is out fishing in the sea, not knowing that a hurricane is coming. His daughter Ikemi and her boyfriend Max must try to save him.

The Beast
by Caroline Walker

'You may see something moving in the corner of your eye. If you turn to look, there will be nothing there.' In Wales, Susie meets the 'undead'. Is it a man, or an animal?

Level 4

The Fruitcake Special and other stories
by Frank Brennan

Five stories about discovery – a perfume that attracts men, a book that shows people's thoughts, a change in an old woman's life, the secret of intelligence and a way of making time stand still.

The Lady in White
by Colin Campbell

John is a TV producer who comes across a story about a ghostly hitch-hiker. He finds out that they have very similar lives and begins to worry about his family and that he may be going mad.

The University Murders
by Richard MacAndrew

Billy Marr claims he has murdered someone in an Edinburgh park. Inspector Logan and Sergeant Grant don't believe him. But then a young woman is found dead in the park. Perhaps Billy is not so innocent . . .

High Life, Low Life
by Alan Battersby

A meeting with a homeless woman and a surprise telephone call takes private investigator Nat Marley through some of the richest and poorest parts of New York.